Shadow Art

Shadow Art

**How to
have fun in the dark
Create 100 shadow
animals**

Sophie Collins

METRO BOOKS
NEW YORK

This book was conceived,
designed, and produced by
iBall, an imprint of **Ivy Press**
210 High Street,
Lewes, East Sussex
BN7 2NS, U.K.

Creative Director **Peter Bridgewater**
Publisher **Jason Hook**
Editorial Director **Caroline Earle**
Senior Project Editor **Dominique Page**
Art Director **Sarah Howerd**
Project Designer **Joanna Clinch**
Page Make-up **Lyndsey Harwood**
Illustrator **John Woodcock**

Metro Books
122 Fifth Avenue
New York, NY 10011

ISBN: 978-0-7607-9100-4

Printed in China

10 9 8 7 6 5 4 3

Contents

6 Introduction to Shadow Art

8 How to Show Your Shadows

10 Hand and Finger Exercises

12 Practicing Basic Shapes

15 **The Animals**

17 Single-hand Animals

37 Two-hand Animals

123 Challenging Animals

195 Advanced Animals

225 **Extending Your Repertoire**

227 Sound Effects and Scenery

269 Human Characters

286 Index and Resources

Introduction to Shadow Art

Making shadow animals is a great pastime. With just a small amount of flexibility, a flashlight (or a couple of light sources, if you want to get more elaborate), and at least one pair of hands, you can create a farmyard full of animals. First made popular a century and a half ago, before radio, television, DVDs, or computer games, hand shadows appeared in many manuals of polite entertainment. One children's encyclopedia published in 1901 claims that "any clever boy or girl" should be able to put on a shadow show of half an hour or so for their friends and relations, and makes suggestions for several playlets, from *Punch and Judy* to the *Babes in the Wood*.

Making shadows a hundred years ago: the surroundings look solemn and the shadow-caster is formally clad—but the wolf on the screen is just the same as the one you will find in this menagerie.

Of course you might not want to go so far, but even in its simplest form there's something compulsive about shadow-casting—first, using just a flashlight, you might try an easy horse or dog shape, then, encouraged by the surprisingly lifelike results, progress to a leaping squirrel or a hopping rabbit. You'll find that you become competitive with family and friends— "That's your pig? Wait till you see my turkey!", and soon you'll be making the sounds that go along with the animals. Shadow art is a great diversion for little kids around bedtime, and a way of luring older ones away from their constant console-tapping; they just won't be able to resist demonstrating how they can get a better result than you.

Shadow Art contains all you need to become an impressive shadow artist. First comes advice and guidance on how to create and show your shadows. Then you will find one hundred animal shapes, graded by difficulty. When you've got through all the easy ones, move on to the moderates—and, when you have all those mastered, flex your fingers, flap your wrists, and have a shot at the rhinoceros, the peacock, or the mole. This is inclusive entertainment—even the smallest fingers, at one end of the family, or the most arthritic ones, at the other, can master the basic dog, or make a snapping crocodile, and most people will enjoy the challenge of the hardest animals, right at the end of the book. After these basics come the sound effects and scenery, which you will want to use if you are to put on a whole shadow show: props to make a range of noises, and frames easily cut from card that will enable you to put your tiger, cobra, and monkey in the jungle, and your cow, bull, and sheep in the farmyard. Finally there are eight shadow people, to give you even more scope with the stories you can enact.

How to Show Your Shadows

The most basic form of shadow-casting calls for just a darkened room, a flashlight or other light source (although it must be local, and not too diffuse—an angled worklamp is ideal), and a pale wall or other surface, such as a blind, on which to cast your shadows. Most shadow-casters will also want an audience—although there's some personal satisfaction in getting the perfect outline and movement of an elephant's trunk or a gobbling turkey, it will be all the greater if there's someone else there with you to gasp at your achievement, or with whom you can take turns.

Starter method

Start off with a worklamp or a flashlight propped securely with books or on a cushion. It can be placed at any height that it will be comfortable to move your hands in front of. It should cast a clear circle of light onto the wall—around two feet in diameter. This will give you enough space to make the animal shape with a clear margin around it. The shadow cast should be clear-edged and dark. Experiment by holding your hand between the light source and the wall until you find the distance at which your shadow animals will show clearly. You will get the most impressive results by forming your animal first, out of the light, and then moving it, fully formed, into the light.

Performance method

When you've reached the point at which your repertoire is worth boasting about, you can try a slightly more elaborate set-up. Your rapt audience sits on a high-backed couch facing the "screen." You kneel behind the couch, with as many accomplices as you need, ready to hold up your hands in animal form behind the couch back (the line of the back is the base of your "stage." Your primary light source (a lamp or a flashlight) illuminates your hands from behind, so that their shadows are cast on to the wall. If you want two layers of shadow (your elephants marching against a circus background, for instance), then it's time to introduce scenery (*see pages 232–67*). You can place your cardboard frame or prop on a table or other flat surface and put a second light source (a table lamp, for example) behind it, as shown in the diagram. Your animals will appear in darker shadow, with the paler outline of the prop scene behind them.

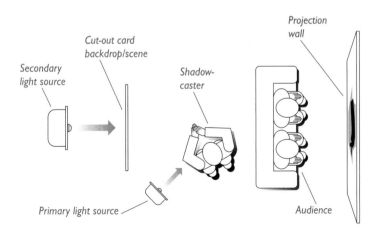

Secondary light source

Cut-out card backdrop/scene

Shadow-caster

Projection wall

Primary light source

Audience

Hand and Finger Exercises

While anyone can make the easiest shadow animals, if you want to manage the whole menagerie you'll need to exercise your hands and fingers. Keen computer games enthusiasts may find that they have an advantage here, and that their fingers are already very flexible. If your hands are stiff, however, run them through a quick calisthenics class before you start making shapes. A couple of minutes spent stretching and flexing will make even stiff hands much more agile. You will find that you have a leading hand, and may find it easier to use this to make the harder parts of the animals—remember, you can always reverse the animal positions and the directions in which they move if you find it easier to create a shape the other way around.

1 Start by clenching both hands and then extending the fingers and stretching each finger, one by one, to its fullest extent.

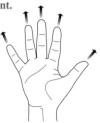

2 Hold your little and your ring finger, and your middle and forefinger together in two pairs, and create a "V"-shaped gap between them, without allowing gaps to appear between the paired fingers.

3 Curl each finger of your right hand into the palm, one by one, while keeping the other fingers stretched straight out. Most people find this easy with their forefinger, but progressively harder moving down the fingers and very hard when they come to the little finger. Repeat until you find it quite easy to do, then run through the same exercise with your left hand.

4 Starting from the little finger and ring finger of your right hand, curl your fingers down to the palm in pairs, while keeping the other fingers stretched straight out (little and ring fingers, ring and middle fingers, middle and forefinger). When you can do this easily, repeat the exercise with your left hand.

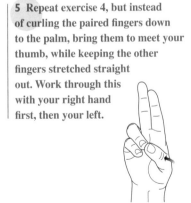

5 Repeat exercise 4, but instead of curling the paired fingers down to the palm, bring them to meet your thumb, while keeping the other fingers stretched straight out. Work through this with your right hand first, then your left.

6 To finish, let both hands hang limply down and circle them half a dozen times, flexing your wrists.

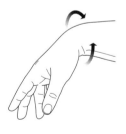

Practicing Basic Shapes

On these pages, we've reproduced three of the simplest animals to make—the German Shepherd dog, the crocodile, and the elephant, with annotation, showing you the order in which to form the shapes, and bend your fingers. Bear in mind that the shapes of people's hands can vary quite dramatically, and that this can make small differences to the final shadows. It may also affect which shapes you find hardest to make—if you have square palms and short fingers, rounded shapes such as the bear cub will be easier for you to do than more attenuated ones like the kangaroo. Keep practicing, and you'll soon identify your favorite shadow animals: those that are easiest for you to make, and most impressive to show.

As you work your way through the menagerie, you'll inevitably find some shadows easier to make than others. Broadly, we've arranged them in the order in which you might try them—from the simplest to the hardest to make. This isn't rigid, though—you might find some that we've cited as "hard" easier to make than you expected. It all depends on the individual shape and flexibility of your hands.

Brace both thumbs upward

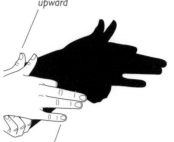

Hold a steady gap between the little finger and the rest of the hand

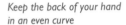
Keep the back of your hand in an even curve

Brace your little finger and forefinger upward, while keeping the trunk pointing steadily down

Hold the bent angle of the fingers as you open and shut your hands

The Animals

Organized in four sections, in order of difficulty, our menagerie consists of one hundred animals, ranging from the humble jellyfish to the haughty camel and the growling grizzly.

Single-Hand Animals

These animals are easiest to make because you only have to worry about the shape and positioning of one hand. Pay close attention to the angle of your hand and arm in relation to the light source, to ensure that your shadow appears straight and clear on the wall.

Swallow

Surely the simplest shadow to make of all. "Swoop" your hand forward in big arcs, moving your paired fingers as you do so to represent the swallow's wings. Keep the thumb braced out as your bird flies, so that the swallow's neck remains outstretched as he darts around.

Goose

This is one of the simplest shadows, and a great starter position. The only possible difficulty you may have is in moving your little finger up and down (to open and shut the beak) without simultaneously moving it in and out. Try thrusting your hand forward and down, then pulling it sharply back, to give the impression of the goose's waddle.

Salamander

The salamander's long, lizardlike head and the draped skin beneath his jaw can be made easily with your left hand. Tuck in your little finger and your thumb as much as is needed to get the silhouette to look just right: this is such a simple shape that it needs to be made quite carefully to give a good impression.

Baby Giraffe

The shadow of the giraffe's calf is formed more simply than the parent's outline (*see pages 70–71*). You can make the giraffe roam around and turn her head by flexing your wrist slightly while "walking" her forward. If you are using prop screens, your giraffe might be placed in the forest (*see pages 240–241*) where she can stretch up her neck and crop the lower leaves and foliage she finds.

Starling

Starlings constantly chatter and shriek, so you can rapidly open and shut the beak of this shadow to make it talk. Pull your little and your ring fingers in, then bend them a bit, and you will find that you are able to make shorter-beaked species, such as sparrows or thrushes. In many nineteenth-century manuals of what was then called "shadowgraphy," this easy-to-form silhouette served as an all-purpose, all-species bird shadow.

Duck

The duck is easy to make. Scissor your fingers for a quacking duck, while making the appropriate sound effect. Raising the head sharply, as shown, while quacking loudly, allows the duck to sound the alarm—perhaps as one of the predator species moves too close for comfort.

Greyhound

If you have short-fingered hands you will be able to form the most recognizable greyhound head. If you have longer fingers, therefore creating a face that looks too elongated, angle your hand slightly toward the wall: this will shorten the dog's nose a little. If you can, also angle your thumb toward the wall a fraction, to make a suitably narrow ear for a sighthound.

Snake

This is a very straightforward silhouette to form: the snake's flickering tongue is made from two blades of grass or tiny slips of paper tucked between the middle and forefinger of the left hand. You can move your whole arm sharply forward to make the snake "strike."

Monkey

You use only your left hand to make the monkey, but it is difficult to fold your knuckles and fingers tidily to make the hunched shape of his head and shoulder convincing, and you may need to practice for a while to get the right silhouette. Use the heel of your hand and the curve of your forearm to make the monkey's lower body.

Two-Hand Animals

The animals in this section use both hands, but are relatively simple to make. You will find that some of them look most lifelike if you hold them still; others, however, will spring into life if you move your conjoined hands in a suitable way—snapping for the crocodile, say, and lowering and extending the neck for the swan.

Shark

The shark's menacing dorsal fin is one of the simplest shadows of all to cast, but you will need a solid base to act as the still surface of the sea—or, if your shark is gliding through choppier waters, you can use the waves frame in the scenery section (*see pages 252–253*). You can teach the smallest child this shadow, so it's a useful addition to the repertoire for a family or group shadow session. Tilt the conjoined hands backward a little as you move the shark forward through the water. Even if you can resist humming the theme tune for the movie *Jaws* as you do so, your audience is unlikely to show such restraint.

Jellyfish

 The jellyfish is quite simple to make, and, if you wobble all the downward-facing fingers slightly as you move it forward, is also a very convincing swimmer.

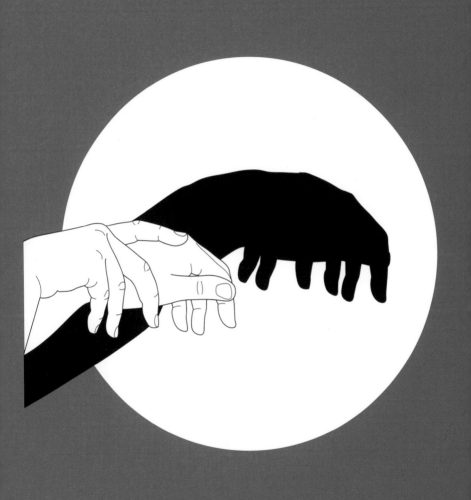

Dove

This is one of the simplest shapes of all. Overlap your thumbs a little to give the bird both a head and a beak. The dove is usually seen in flight, an effect that is achieved by flapping both your hands to and fro, but it must fly in a straight line—if it soars, the illusion will be spoiled by too much of your forearms becoming visible.

German Shepherd

As its name suggests, the German Shepherd dog is a herding breed. This shadow is extremely easy to do: if you keep the mouth open, your dog will have a fierce, intent look; close it for a gentler, more reflective profile.

Billy Goat

The billy goat has prominent horns, a long profile, and, like the nanny goat (*see pages 184–185*), a small, neat beard. This is a simpler shadow to make than that of the nanny goat, and it has an unsophisticated look. Nonetheless, as part of a farmyard scene it can work surprisingly well.

Horse

This simple outline can look surprisingly equine, provided you get the angle between your thumbs and palms right for the horse's head. Practice moving the little finger of your right hand up and down, so that your shadow horse can open and shut its mouth, while keeping the lower two fingers of your left hand tucked away behind your right palm, in order to keep the silhouette clear and clean.

Crab

The crab is a very easy shadow to form. As soon as you have a realistic outline, make your crab move by shuffling it rapidly sideways, moving all its legs at once, and hiding your forearms behind the stage edge.

Weasel

Experiment with the angle of the raised fingers of your right hand to give your weasel a sufficiently narrow and flexible-looking head and neck. Smooth out the knuckles of your left hand as far as possible to make a smooth, supple back. Your extended thumb makes the weasel's tail, which will be tilted slightly upright as it runs forward.

Armadillo

The ridged back of the armadillo gives it its character. This is a simple shadow to make, but experiment with the placement of your right hand—the knuckles must be held low enough to make ridges rather than humps. Gentle movements of the fingers of your left hand will open and shut the armadillo's mouth as he moves slowly forward.

Swan

The swan is one of the most elegant shadow silhouettes, and you can "sail" it along the back of your stage edge in a very stately manner. The right hand, forming the wing, should disappear behind your left upper arm at the wrist, so that your swan shadow doesn't have any breaks in its overall outline.

Crocodile

Snippety-snap! The crocodile can be made to snap his jaws simply by opening and closing your hands sharply. Move your hands across your stage from left to right as you do so, making a snapping noise.

Snail

The simple snail is easily made. Because the shape involves both your forearms as well as your hands, you will need to move your whole body in order for it to slither across the picture. Practice sliding over whichever high surface forms your "stage" edge, while still holding the snail shadow. Wave the eye-stalks a little as your snail moves.

Bear Cub

In contrast to the fierce-looking adult bear (*see pages 128–129*), the bear cub has a soft, blunt face, with its ears pricked up in curiosity. The top of the head is easily made with a clenched left hand, while the bear cub's muzzle is formed by the flattened fingers of your right hand, carefully angled into position. Try slowly turning your left hand to make your bear cub's ears move.

Ostrich

The ostrich is formed in a way that is very similar to the swan (*see pages 56–57*), except that your left forearm should be held rather more upright to make a straighter neck. The ostrich's bulky tail feathers are made by draping a light piece of cloth (anything that will make bulk, but without having too much weight) over your upper left arm and, if necessary, holding it up into a realistically puffy shape with your right hand, as seen in the picture.

Hermit Crab

The hermit crab has a scuttling, sideways gait, rushing forward in short bursts, and then pausing for a moment before making another forward rush. Practice holding your left hand over your right (forming the hermit crab's shell) and moving it along simultaneously with the "legs," which are created by your right fingers, to make the movement of the crab convincing.

Roosting Hen

The hen portrayed here is sitting on her nest, and is an easy shape to imitate. To make her move, tuck the thumb of your right hand behind the heel of your left (as seen here, it's forming the edge of her nest) and move the hen forward in a slightly jerky motion, as though she were strutting her way across the farmyard.

Giraffe

Your right hand should be held in as clean a line as possible so that the giraffe's neck looks smooth and doesn't have any bumps. Raise the knuckle of the forefinger of your left hand to give the giraffe his eye bump. Practice wiggling the fingers of your left hand very slightly so that the head can dip forward and the nose can twitch a little as the giraffe's neck sways forward.

Jackal

The jackal has a rather doglike head, but also a mane of fur that runs along the center line of his back, giving the appearance of permanently raised hackles. The mane is created with the knuckles of your right hand, ranged down the neck (your left wrist) of your shadow shape.

Porcupine

This is an easy outline, in which the slightly tucked fingers of your right hand form the characteristic quills. You can turn the porcupine a little by moving the fingers of your left hand (which make his head and face), but keep the overlap between the hands consistent, or you will find that the shadow head suddenly parts from the body.

Penguin

You will need to arch the back of your right hand and your wrist to make the long, deep, rounded breast of the penguin. The beak points down, and the eye is made from a small gap between the middle and forefinger of your left hand. Tip both hands forward then move them slowly and laboriously forward to imitate the penguin's shuffling walk.

Skunk

Anyone who liked cartoons as a child will remember the luxuriantly thick tail of the skunk, carried high over his back and fluffed out like a bush. The shadow skunk is no exception—his tail looms over his comparatively slight profile and is arranged in thick puffs by the knuckles and second joints of the fingers of your left hand. You can make your shadow skunk chatter by quickly overlapping and then separating the little and ring fingers of your right hand, which form his small snout and mouth.

Parrot

The parrot has a higher, more dome-shaped head than the other birds, and a deeper curved beak. This is a straightforward shadow to form—experiment with your flexibility by getting your parrot to pick up individual peanuts from a small dish on the "stage" with its beak. When he is holding a peanut, you can throw his head back and he can appear to swallow it (you will actually be dropping it behind the cover of your forearm).

Fawn

The fawn has a large, startled eye, with the emotion expressed by his large pupil—keep your little finger in a straight line, bisecting the eye neatly to achieve the correct shape. The small, upright tail can be shaken sharply, in the manner of baby animals, as the fawn moves forward.

Rat

Although your right hand supports your left and helps you to broaden the rat's neck, this is essentially a one-hand shadow, and is not particularly difficult to make. Slips of paper or blades of grass act as effective whiskers and will twitch realistically as you move your middle and ring fingers slightly to and fro so that the rat wiggles his nose.

Red Deer

The red deer is distinguished by his imposing antlers, which are easy to form with the fingers of your right hand. If you practice with a friend, you can make your shadow stags fight realistically by lowering their heads and horns, then moving them sharply toward one another, and letting their antlers "clash."

Roe Deer

The roe deer's strongest characteristics are its long, oval eye, and its horns, which are angled well forward in front of its ear. This is one of those shadows that is easy to approximate but quite hard to get perfect. Practice in order to balance the shape correctly. Like the other deer species, when you've made a lifelike roe deer, you can make her graze by plucking up small, previously gathered tufts of grass.

Turkey

The turkey is harder to make than it looks. Your left hand should be kept well tucked under your right, with the thumb held in under the palm. When you have a shadow that looks like a turkey, try wobbling the lowered fingers of your left hand so that the turkey's wattles shake as it moves forward. Make a gobbling sound for added realism.

Bull

The finger shape for the bull is similar to that of the cow (*see pages 94–95*), but the bull has a blunter face and more strongly curved horns. If you'd like your bull to wear a ring through his nose all you need to do is twist a paperclip into a neat circle and fix it at a slight angle—so that it reflects as a ring, and not simply as a line—between the middle and forefinger of your right hand.

Cow

This is a simple silhouette, but you may find it quite hard at first to curl your left thumb round flexibly to make the cow's second horn. Practice bending and rotating both thumbs in as full a circle as you can.

Water Buffalo

The water buffalo is formed in a manner similar to that of the bull (*see pages 92–93*) but his wider, curving horns are made by curling the thumb and forefinger of your left hand strongly outward. This is one shadow in which longer fingers will have the advantage—you will be able to get a more impressive spread and breadth for the buffalo's horns. As with the bull shadow, you can make a ring to lead the buffalo with a paperclip bent into a ring, or a readymade curtain ring, inserted between the middle and forefinger of your right hand. You can even tie a string to it, so that your buffalo can be led.

Turtle

Strong flippers and a blunt head characterize the turtle. Your left forefinger creates the turtle's face, while the fingers of each hand are flexed together for the flippers. The heels of both your hands must be pushed outward into a curve to form the shadow of the shell. Once formed, it's easy to make your shadow turtle swim—simply move the flippers to and fro with deep movements to indicate the animal's confidence in the water.

Spider

The spider is quite an easy shadow to create but it is somewhat challenging to move in a realistic way.

Having overlapped your hands and bent your fingers to match the picture opposite, you should move all of your fingers together, angling your hands so that your spider appears to be scuttling forward, rather than sideways, which would be the more natural movement, and the one that you would use if making the shadow crab (*see pages 50–51*).

Albatross

The impressive head of the albatross is balanced by the shape of its strong wing—which, like that of the raven (*see pages 108–109*), is made by reflecting your left hand face-on to the wall. Adjust the angle of your hands to one another until the wing appears to be part of the bird. You can settle the albatross on a "branch" (the couch back), and flap its head and wing strongly, imitating the way in which seabirds shake themselves off after they emerge from the water.

Fox

The fox is not a particularly difficult shadow to make, but the fingers of your left hand should be overlapped as much as necessary to make his face as pointed as possible, or you will find that the resulting creature looks more horselike than vulpine. You should keep your thumbs angled, too, until the fox's ears are realistically pointed.

Butterfly

The butterfly is a flapping shadow that can fly across your shadow stage with broad, generous movements as you open and close your hands. It may take a few practice sessions to keep the tiny strips of paper that make the antennae in place when the butterfly is in active flight. If you are accomplished at "opening" the four fingers of each hand into two pairs, you can give your butterfly paired wings, which will make the silhouette more authentic.

Raven

The raven's silhouette is much more hunched and less open than that of the dove (*see pages 42–43*); it is portrayed while huddled on a branch, rather than in full flight. The head and upper body are formed with a curled right hand, while the left hand is held open and flat, so that the raven can stretch out one of its wings.

Toad

As you might expect, the toad is formed in a similar way to the frog (*see pages 118–119*), but with a more pronounced eye hump and a deeper, smoother throat (for a lower, bass croak). Round out the back of your right hand down to the wrist to swell the throat, and then bring it in again, making a croaking noise as the toad "exhales."

Pigeon

Make sure that your forearms overlap sufficiently for there to be no gap in the shadow shape of the pigeon's breast. If you open the curled fingers of your left hand very slightly while jerking both arms forward a little, the pigeon can be made to form a characteristic pecking motion. Be careful to maintain the distance of your thumb from your left palm, so that the eye stays in place as you move.

Hippopotamus

If you have long, slender hands, you may need to fold in the fingers of your left hand rather than keep the palm and fingers flat, as shown, to give your hippopotamus a convincingly blunt lower jaw. Although this is a comparatively simple shape to form, it demands that your left hand be flexible and may take more practice than you expect. Open and shut the hippopotamus's jaws and roar loudly to complete the fearsome impression.

Moose

The moose is very similar to that of the red deer (*see pages 86–87*), but the upper hand is curved more, so that the palm of your left hand gives the impression of the broader areas of a moose's antlers. The moose's complex upper mouth and jaw are formed by keeping the fingers of your right hand overlapping rather than even at the ends.

Frog

The frog's throat needs to be held in a smooth curve, with a soft angle where your right hand meets your wrist. Use your top (left) hand to open and shut the mouth, relaxing your lower hand a little to create a swell in the frog's neck. Make a throaty croaking noise as you move the mouth, and "hop" your frog across the frame by jumping both hands simultaneously, holding the shape in place as you do so.

Alpaca

Alpacas have a ball of wool, which looks somewhat like a pompon, growing on top of their head between their ears, giving them a very different profile from that of the llama (*see pages 138–139*). This shadow clearly shows the bulk between the ears of the alpaca, as well as the slightly hunched back, although not humped dramatically like that of a camel—just a little rounded.

Challenging Animals

The intermediate members of the menagerie, some of these shadows will take a little practice to make effectively. Be patient and work your way through them — when you can form all the animals in this section, you're well on your way to becoming a shadow virtuoso.

Rabbit

The rabbit's long ears and whiffling nose are his most characteristic features, and you can easily give the impression of both with this shadow. Bend the two upright fingers of your right hand at the knuckle, then jerk them upright again to make the rabbit sense a distraction, while moving the three lowered fingers of your left hand to and fro very slightly to make your rabbit's nose twitch with anticipation. Keep the ear movements abrupt and the nose movements subtle to create the most realistic-looking shadow rabbit.

Leopard

Leopards are usually found sitting high in the trees, resting and waiting for prey. The intelligent profile of this beast is poised on a long neck as it looks down through the branches around its perch. You can turn the leopard's head by making tiny movements of the joined fingers of your left hand, while keeping your right hand still.

Bear

The growling bear's shadow shows ears, gaping jaws, and front and back legs, so you need to place your individual fingers carefully to make a balanced shape. Tuck your right thumb neatly behind your left hand, and form the head and ears first. When you have the pointed ears and the face shape, use the thumb of your left hand to make the lower leg, and the little and ring fingers to make the foreleg. This is a shadow that doesn't move—if you want it to walk, make the head only, and move the shadow down so that the lower parts of your hands are concealed behind the surface (couch back or equivalent) that you are using as your stage "floor."

Pig

The hardest aspect of making the pig is extending the little and ring fingers of your right hand just the correct amount to give the impression of the pig's little legs and trotters. Also, the throat needs to have a smooth curve up to the snout for your hand shadow to look sufficiently porcine. A little practice will ensure that you achieve a properly piglike outline. Snort and snuffle through your nose, and move your "leg" fingers lightly to and fro to make the pig trot forward.

Elephant

Keep the crevice in the right hand tiny—it forms the elephant's small but characterful eye. The trunk can be upraised (with accompanying trumpeting sound) by turning your left hand the other way up and curling your ring finger upward, but you can't do this as the elephant is progressing magisterially—you will have to withdraw your hands and then re-form the head. Practice doing this quickly so that the gap in your performance isn't noticeable.

Crow

A short, blunt tail and a strong outline make the crow instantly recognizable. He makes a good shadow to include in a woodland scene, perhaps observing while the dove and the swallow (*see pages 42–43 and 18–19*), which are both easier shadows to move, fly to and fro. You can duck the crow's head forward onto his breast and down to his side if you like, to create the impression that he is grooming his feathers.

Vulture

This scavenging bird looks like no other, and the hunched shoulders and powerful beak make its shadow rendition instantly recognizable. Getting your fingers into position is straightforward, but keeping the beak in place while forming your fingers into the "hump" of the back is harder; it's easiest to make the bird in two parts—positioning each hand separately—and then putting them together.

Llama

The llama's face is raised and its ears are alert. This creature is formed in a similar way to the head of the peacock (*see pages 144–145*), but with a wider, smoother chest (and, of course, no tail!). Crook the middle and little fingers of your right hand to move the llama's face.

Possum

The possum has long ears, a sharp, pointed profile, and strong jaws. The challenge of this particular shadow lies not in the positioning of your hands but in the angle of their position between the light source and your screen. If you find the shadow doesn't look like the one in the picture, swivel your conjoined hands slightly round to the right and you should find that your shadow falls into shape.

Cockatoo

The cockatoo is not a difficult shadow to make, but its shape is rather inflexible once formed—you will find that you can open and close the beak, but it takes far more practice to move the bird around without ruffling its crest and spoiling the outline of the shadow.

Peacock

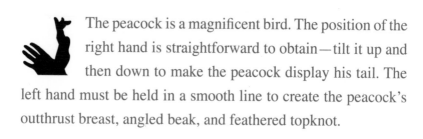

The peacock is a magnificent bird. The position of the right hand is straightforward to obtain—tilt it up and then down to make the peacock display his tail. The left hand must be held in a smooth line to create the peacock's outthrust breast, angled beak, and feathered topknot.

Bulldog

The bulldog has a rounded, blunt face and a keen, triangular eye. The most difficult aspect of forming this shadow is keeping the join between the upper part of the face and the muzzle smooth; tuck the fingertips of your left hand in between the knuckles of your right to make the shadow look convincing and all-of-a-piece.

Wild Boar

The wild boar's fierce profile is quite different from the gentle curves of the domestic pig. The tusk is made by flexing the forefinger of your left hand strongly upward. A small, slightly mean-looking eye adds to the overall predatory appearance, and you can make the long snout twitch by moving the middle, ring, and little fingers of the left hand, being careful to keep them together as you do so.

Sea Cow

Manatees, or sea cows, like walruses, have complex, wrinkled faces which, at first glance, appear to have several sets of lips! The sea cow's rounded head and pouting profile are created by interlocking your hands and extending the thumb and forefinger of your left hand through the gaps. Raise the sea cow's head and wriggle his top lip while making a snorting, bellowing noise for real authenticity.

Cougar

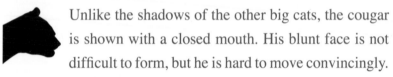 Unlike the shadows of the other big cats, the cougar is shown with a closed mouth. His blunt face is not difficult to form, but he is hard to move convincingly. If your cougar is intently watching the shadow of some potential prey—a rabbit, for instance—then you can establish his fierce concentration by pushing the thumb of your left hand forward with tiny movements to convey the twitching of his ears.

Owl

Large, round eyes make this simple shadow instantly recognizable as that of an owl—and you can open and close the owl's eyes with slight movements of the thumbs and forefingers of both your hands. Practice until you can move them simultaneously, or open and close just one to make your owl blink. The owl's small upright ears are positioned at the corners of his head, and are formed by gently angling your little fingers inward.

Anteater

The anteater has a very characteristic movement of the head—he walks forward with his long nose extended, then pauses and does a sweep from side to side looking for his next meal of ants or other insects. As you move his head, straighten out his nose a little, keeping your hands carefully together, then move them slowly from left to right before resuming your anteater's forward motion.

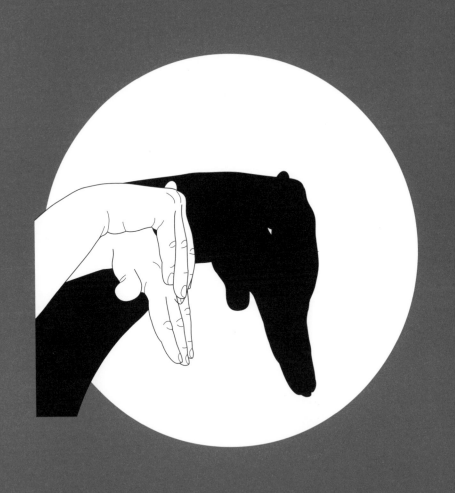

King Cobra

The king cobra is formed in a way very similar to that of the ordinary snake (*see pages 32–33*), but your right hand is called into play to give the ruler of the snake world a fittingly impressive hood. It can be tricky to get the grip across your left wrist fashioned to make the hood broad enough, so practice until your cobra looks realistic whether he is simply standing and swaying, hood outstretched, or leaning forward ready to strike.

Mole

To make a convincing mole shadow is more difficult than it looks. The overall outline is made in a similar way to that of the pig (*see pages 130–131*), but with a shallower, smoother head, a longer, less defined snout and short flipperlike paws. The two fingers forming the snout can be moved slightly to make the mole's nose "twitch" as it is raised above the earth. Rather than moving from left to right, your mole shadow should emerge from the stage vertically, just like a real mole digging itself out of the soil.

Eagle

Creating the eagle shadow involves your forearms as well as your hands, so practice overlapping them easily before you try to interlock your fingers to form the eagle's head and beak. The forefinger of your right hand needs to be sharply crooked in order to give the bird the requisite fierce, predatory look.

Hare

It's easy to wiggle the hare's expressive ears, but making the shadow jump is more difficult. Practice pulling the thumb of your left hand sharply down, then "leaping" your joined hands upward while returning your thumb to a horizontal position. Managing this while keeping the forelegs in place and without either enlarging or losing the tiny gap in your fingers which makes the eye poses quite a challenge, and one that you may need a little time to get right.

Sheep

The sheep is harder to make than it looks—the nose needs to be quite blunt and the mouth open just the right amount to give a properly sheeplike impression. Tuck the middle finger of your right hand down at a sharp angle to make the eye the correct shape. When you've mastered the outline, make your sheep graze and baa by lowering and raising the head and opening and closing the mouth.

Antelope

The antelope has an extended snout and tall horns. Keep the thumb of your right hand and the little finger of your left tucked well in and down, out of sight, to ensure you achieve a good, clean shadow outline. Tilt both hands forward and down to make the antelope "graze"— you can even let him pull up a tuft of previously picked grass, tucked neatly between the ring and little fingers of your right hand for added verisimilitude.

Kangaroo

The kangaroo shadow doesn't require any particular flexibility in your fingers, and the hand positions are not at all complex, but you will certainly need to experiment to get the relative angles of the head, tail, and legs just right. The longer your fingers, the easier you will find this shadow to make—but, given time, it is possible for even the short-fingered to achieve a convincing result!

Tapir

Tapirs have long, mobile noses and surprisingly heavy lower jaws. The tapir shadow is a modified form of the elephant shadow (*see pages 132–133*). Keep the eye small, and move the angled thumb of your left hand up and down a little while wiggling your left fingers to make the tapir snuffle realistically along the forest floor.

Badger

Badgers tend to sniff around the ground as they walk, and bending the conjoined middle and forefinger of your left hand will give you a similar effect. The shape is not difficult to make, but moving your fingers in pairs to enable your badger to walk naturally is hard; keep practicing until the movement no longer looks wooden.

Tortoise

This is a simple shape to form, but another one that it is hard to move realistically. The tortoise can be made to walk forward in the authentic, lumbering manner by moving each leg forward, one at a time. This is a good shadow to use to practice movement, as even relatively stiff fingers can eventually be formed into a very realistic motion.

Donkey

The challenge of this shadow is to make a neat little gap between the ring and little fingers of your right hand for the donkey's eye, while keeping all the fingers of your left hand neatly tucked in to give it a solid, convincing nose. When you've mastered the shape, see if you can fling his head back and open his mouth (separating the little and ring fingers of your left hand) to make the donkey bray.

Lyre Bird

 His extravagant tail is the identifying characteristic of the lyre bird, and it takes all eight fingers of both hands to render it convincingly. The head is made from your right thumb, bent a little to give the impression of the bird's neck and crop. A long slender thumb will make a more believable shadow than a short, blunt one—if you are not blessed with long fingers, concentrate on making the lyre bird's tail as impressive as possible!

Chameleon

Balanced across a branch, the chameleon has curled his tail in underneath his perch. The arched back and peering, inquisitive face can be moved a little, but it is hard to keep your hands held in the correct position to make him move all at once. Curl and uncurl his tail by moving your left thumb, and turn the joined fingers of your right hand to and fro a little to make the chameleon turn his head.

Nanny Goat

Keep the curve of the nanny goat's profile smooth, with only a slight angle where your right hand makes contact with your left. The nanny goat's horns point well forward, with a small, raised ear formed by your thumb behind them. The beard is an especially expressive feature, and you can make it wag by flexing your little finger to and fro.

Woodpecker

As you would expect, the woodpecker has a powerful beak. The long, forked tail descends below the branch on which it sits. If you have a stable upright that you can use as a tree trunk, you can imitate the action of the bird by rapidly advancing and withdrawing the beak against the trunk, making the characteristic "hammering" peck. Keep your left hand still and use your right to show the woodpecker at work.

Cat

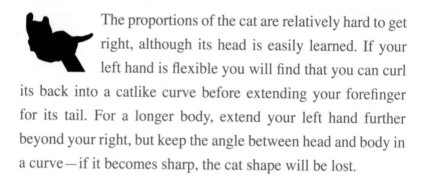

The proportions of the cat are relatively hard to get right, although its head is easily learned. If your left hand is flexible you will find that you can curl its back into a catlike curve before extending your forefinger for its tail. For a longer body, extend your left hand further beyond your right, but keep the angle between head and body in a curve—if it becomes sharp, the cat shape will be lost.

Cockerel

The bottom half of the cockerel's head is formed like that of the turkey (*see pages 90–91*), but the crest is made by tilting three fingers of the left hand upward, instead of folding them across the top of the head. You need flexible fingers and plenty of practice to get all the angles right and to make the cockerel appear lifelike.

Marmot

The marmot is formed in a way very similar to that of the hare (*see pages 164–165*), but with a simpler head and a slightly domed skull. The eye is created by leaving a tiny gap between the middle and forefinger of the left hand. If your fingers are flexible enough you can make the marmot move his forepaws prior to him "hopping" away (marmots move in little leaps).

Advanced Animals

This group of animals demands great flexibility in your fingers, hands, and wrists, and the ability not only to make but also to hold an awkward position in order to achieve a satisfactory shadow. Be prepared to practice—the results will be worth it.

Wolf

 The wolf has a narrow, intense eye and open, menacing jaws. Practice keeping the pupil in place as you move the wolf forward. In time, you can learn to open and shut the toothy jaws, although at first you will find it hard to keep your paired fingers crossed as you do so.

Coyote

The coyote's jaw is formed in the same way as that of the wolf (*see pages 196–197*), but it has a bonier, more elongated head, formed by the ridges of the knuckles of your right hand. Its ears are long, and angled forward. You can make it howl by tilting the whole head upward and vibrating (rather than closing) the jaws. At first you will find it hard to move the head while keeping your paired fingers crossed, but eventually you will be able to do so quite easily.

Mouse

Getting all of your fingers into the correct alignment to make the mouse is hard, but this shadow is worth practicing, as it is one of the most lifelike of all in movement—just wriggle the extended finger of your left hand to wave the tail while crooking the little finger of your right to "walk" the front leg forward. If you are finding the shadow very difficult, try making the mouse at first without the eye—this will allow you to hold your hand more loosely. Do take the trouble to add tiny straw or paper whiskers, though, as they will add greatly to the impression of "mouse."

Rhinoceros

A long blunt nose with a central tusk or horn characterizes the rhinoceros, and this is made by extending the little finger of the right hand beyond the slightly curled fingers of the left. The trick is to angle your little finger against the light in such a way as to thicken the appearance of the horn; if you point it away from the light and toward the wall just a bit you will find that the resulting horn is satisfactorily hefty to match the animal's fearsome reputation.

Tiger

To create the tiger you will need a cloth or towel that you can drape right around both wrists to form the ear and the neck, as shown. Practice by first getting the drape of the fabric in place, then moving your hands gently into position to form the tiger's authentically toothy profile.

Lion

 Forming the strong profile of the lion shadow requires the same hand positioning as that of the tiger (*see pages 204–205*), with the addition of a flowing mane. The lion's mane is achieved by taking a length of fabric (towel, T-shirt, or rumpled cotton shirt—anything will serve provided that it is light enough to be draped to give it some volume) and wrapping it around your wrists and the top of your left hand, rumpling it to give it the appearance of waves. You will need a helper to arrange the cloth after you have placed your hands.

Jaguar

The jaguar is formed in a similar way to the panther (*see pages 220–221*), but has a blunter nose, which looks slightly wrinkled. You could make a low snarl to match its appearance, poised to strike on some unwary prey. The fingers of your right hand must be neatly aligned to give the muzzle a realistic line, and you should keep the ear small and swiveled forward to match the animal's concentration.

Squirrel

When you have mastered this realistic squirrel it can be made to leap along an angled branch if you have one you can use as a prop. Create the lifelike small "jumping" movements with the little finger and thumb of your left hand as you curl and uncurl the little finger of your right hand. You need a very flexible right hand and wrist to get the shape just right; if you have difficulty, try flexing and circling your wrists a few times and then try again.

Sea Anemone

The sea anemone need only gently move its arms once it is formed, but it requires extremely flexible fingers to make — try bending your fingers to and fro in twos before attempting to make the four conjoined pairs of arms that give the anemone its characteristic outline.

Pug Dog

At first glance this is a simple shadow, but when you try it, you will find that this particular combination of curled and straight fingers is far more challenging than it looks. Practice the positions in which your hands are held separately before you try to put them together. The perky tail of the pug must be matched by an appropriately blunt face at the opposite end to make a convincing outline.

Camel

The camel's most characteristic facial feature is a "whiffle" of its double top lip. You can emulate this by wiggling the forefinger of your left hand very slightly when the you have formed the camel's head. Move your conjoined hands jerkily up and down as you walk the camel forward to mimic his swaying gait.

Terrier

The terrier is one of the few shadow animals that is shown complete, with a long back and an eager, upright tail. None of the upright shadows are overly difficult to form in themselves, but obtaining a perfect shadow with mouth, eye, and legs all clearly aligned and in place will certainly take some practice, and moving your terrier is challenging—if you tilt your hands forward a little it can move forward jerkily, but the movement will never be very natural!

Panther

Beasts of prey are easiest to show with aggressively open mouths, waiting to pounce on unsuspecting prey. If you curl the fingers of your right hand in and down slightly you can make your panther snarl (keep any sound effects very low for the best effect—most predators snarl and growl in a quiet, steady note).

Unicorn

For the final animal in our menagerie we have included a mythical beast, so that you have even more scope with the stories you can enact. The head of the unicorn is formed more like those of the deer family than the horse, with a slightly blunter nose than, for example, the antelope. The single horn is made by the middle and forefinger of your left hand, extended to their fullest length, while the ring finger forms the eye.

Extending Your Repertoire

When you are able to make most of the animals in the menagerie, you can master the art of using frames to create separate scenes to suit them, and sound effects for more lifelike portrayals. You may also want to create interactions. These will be more varied if you have human characters to hand, so you will also find a range of shadow people here.

Sound Effects
and Scenery

When you have perfected a number of animal shadows you will most probably find that you want to add sound effects and scenery to create a more impressive performance. Here is some advice on making atmospheric animal noises, plus plenty of backdrops and frames to enable a wide range of stories to be told.

Creating Sound Effects

Sound effects will not only create more of an atmosphere to your shadow "performance" (even if that performance is only a sequence of ten simple animals displayed to a group of thrilled six-year-olds), but you will also find that it's much easier to make the animals move convincingly if you have some sounds to work along with. Don't start too ambitiously—a few self-produced animal sounds attached to the clip-clop of hooves and a watery splash as the hippopotamus moves into view will be impressive enough. If you want to use some props, you will need a second pair of hands. This can be a good way to make even a modest show into a family affair; children are usually enthusiastic helpers, and may find it easier to make the noises than to form the animal shadows, some of which are tricky for smaller hands. Tailor the effects you pick to the age of the child.

Walking noises

You can create many different footfalls by filling three trays—one with gravel, one with cat litter, and one with cornflakes—then setting down different elements in them in a footstep rhythm. The traditional "clopping" of horse's hooves is made with coconut shells crunching into gravel, but small and large cans (both full and empty), and inverted empty mugs and bowls will all make different steps. The heavier the can and the coarser the material it is "walking" on, the heavier the animal it represents.

Alongside walking noises, you may want to represent the sound of grass or foliage being brushed aside. With stalking animals, such as lions and tigers, just this noise may be the most effective—especially if you want the shadow of a jaguar, for instance, to pounce on an antelope. If you rustle and crunch the sweeping part of a straw broom or brush with your hands, it sounds like an animal moving through high grass. The impression of walking through leaves can be created by brushing through the cornflakes in the third of your footstep trays with your spare hand, as you create the "crunch" of the step with your can or mug.

Gravel, cat litter, or cereal will all make different noises

"Walking" coconut shells is a traditional way to make the sound of hooves

The sweeping motion of a brush or broom can imitate the rustle of foliage

Sound chart

Use this chart to match likely sounds to the right animals. Experiment to get the best combinations—for example, you can make an elephant walk across the savannah, then pause to lower and raise his trunk and take a drink, accompanied by a gurgling water sound, while a lighter tread might announce the arrival of an ostrich, and a plunger pushed sharply into a bucket could represent the sudden, fearsome lunge of a crocodile.

Type of sound	How you make it	What you can use it for
Weighty footsteps	Lightly grinding heavy cans into a tray of gravel or small pebbles	Elephants, water buffalo, rhinoceros
Walking over a forest floor, twigs snapping	Cans or an inverted mug or small bowl into a tray of cornflakes	Bears (lighter footfall for a bear cub), moose, or heavier deer
Walking through dry grass in the savannah	Rub the bristles of a brush or broom briskly between your palms	Any animal of the jungles or plains, from elephants to antelope
Walking over snow or sandy desert ground	Cans or an inverted mug or small bowl into a tray of cat litter	Camel, coyote. A sheet of cellophane "rustled" over cat litter sounds like the movement of a snake

Type of sound	How you make it	What you can use it for
Watery snorts	Half-fill a balloon with water, then squeeze it sharply with your hands into a bucket	Hippo, elephant, antelope, or buffalo at the watering hole
Heavy movement in water	A plumber's plunger plunged once or twice into a bucket of water	Hippopotamus, anaconda, or crocodile in water as it leaps up at its prey
Bubbling water	Blow gently through a straw into a full beaker of water	Hippopotamus or sea cow. Good for water dwellers who don't have a sound associated with them, such as jellyfish
Wings in flight	A pair of rubber gloves, rhythmically flapped in the air	Swan, raven. A heavier hand will give you the nonaerial flapping of an ostrich, turkey, or goose
Weather—heavy rain	Rice poured onto a sheet of thin metal or Perspex	Good background to a parade of forest animals, using the "rain" or "storm" prop frames
Weather—thunder	A sheet of thin metal or Perspex shaken rapidly from one side	For "storm" sequences, in between rattling bursts of rain

Using Scenery

When it was explained on pages 8 and 9 how to set up your animal shadows for show, a layer of "background" shadow was mentioned. Essentially, this is just a frame for your animal action—it means that you can set up simple scenarios for your characters. If several people want to make animals simultaneously then this is a great way to create a more complex scene—if you use a jungle background, for example, a parrot might be pecking high up on a branch, while the elephant and the tiger have a snarling confrontation below. Or a monkey could be sitting at the base of a tree while a lion watches his potential prey from a distance. We have supplied 17 variations here, giving you endless scope for invention.

To use the frames, you should enlarge them on a photocopier (how large you need them to be depends on the distance of your secondary light source from the wall, and on how pale you want the background frame to be, so experiment by holding differently sized rectangles of paper in front of the light source and seeing what size they are reflected on the wall). Enlarge your chosen image to the right size, trace it on an appropriately sized piece of light card, and cut the center of the frame out. In pictures in which there are independent elements (for example, moon and stars) make sure that you don't cut through the strips of card by which they are suspended.

Combining scenes

Some of the frames we show here can be combined—for example, you could pair the stormy seas frame with the moon and stars. The simplest is the arcade, which is just a basic framework of arches; this scene would be a good choice to practice with, as it will give you an idea of the relative strengths of shadow you need to give the impression of an overall scene while simultaneously keeping your animal outlines clear and easy to see.

If you want to use a sequence of scenes—and, to do so, you'll probably be creating an increasingly ambitious shadow show—cut a sheet of solid cardboard to the same size as the outer edge of your frames, and hold it up between frames so that you can make a clean transition between your pictures. This will keep your pictures clear and separate.

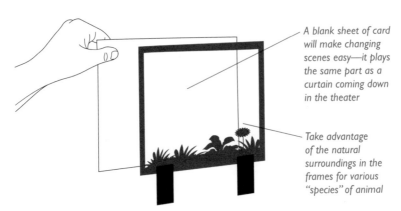

A blank sheet of card will make changing scenes easy—it plays the same part as a curtain coming down in the theater

Take advantage of the natural surroundings in the frames for various "species" of animal

Arcade

This is a simple effect, and a good frame for you to practice with. The arcade consists of three arches, within which your shadow animals can stand framed, through which they can progress, or in which they can meet. This easy device can bring the most unlikely animals together, and acts as an effective frame for any or all of them.

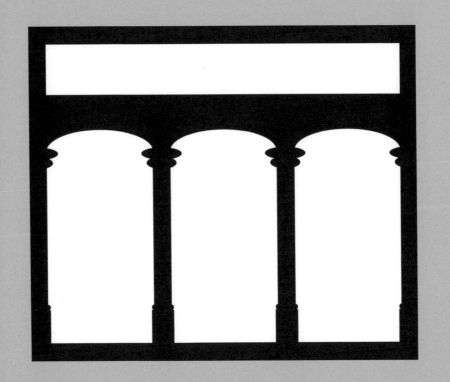

Trees

This frame offers you two basic tree shapes, one with a branch for shadow animals to "perch" on if you want to create an animal scene. The squirrel might rest momentarily before jumping back down to the ground, and the dove could be seen taking off from the branch. It would also make a good roost for the woodpecker.

Hills

A landscape of rolling hills makes an effective backdrop for any of the grazing animals, from the sheep to the various sorts of deer, although this is strictly a backdrop, as it has no specific features with which your created animals can interact. It is, however, a good practice frame for ensuring that the two layers of shadows you are making—one background, one active—have the right relative density.

Forest

This frame portrays a deciduous forest. The tree stump to the left of the picture could be a good pausing point for some of the smaller animals—the mouse, the rat, and even the spider could all be seen climbing onto and over it, although perhaps not simultaneously, as the difference in scale would be too pronounced.

Tropical Jungle

In the tropics there is less ground cover, but the dense canopy of trees drips with hanging lianas and vines. A monkey may sit thinking on the forest floor, first spied on by a tiger or a cougar, then interrupted by the slow, majestic passage of an elephant. Use the jungle as a backdrop for some of your most exotic species of shadow animals.

Desert

Two palm trees lean in, one from each side, over the undulating dunes. You may want to enlist some friends and create a whole caravan of camels, or simply concentrate on making your own camel outline process from one side of the screen to the other with its characteristic swaying gait. You can lay one frame on top of another to create a moonlit night in the desert, to change the mood.

Seashore

Calm sea is bordered by a steep cliff that is topped by a lighthouse. A sea cow's head may pop over the horizon, or the fin of a shark may be seen just above the waterline. A storm at sea can be created by overlaying the scene with another, showing heavy clouds and a lightning bolt. As the storm dies down, a crab could scuttle along the shoreline in search of debris cast up by wild seas.

Circus

A basic Big Top shape forms the frame for a shadow circus scenario. Two simple drums offer posing places to a whole host of potential performing shadows — the giraffe and her baby might take a turn around the ring, followed by the performing horses and an elephant or two. You can create circus headdresses for some animals with one or two curling feathers held between your knuckles.

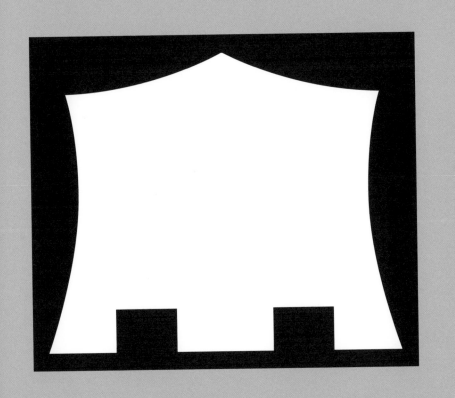

Farmyard

The farmyard frame offers a habitat for all the farm animals you have learned to make. Hen, goat, sheep, turkey, goose, cow, and bull will all be at home here. You can make one or two animals roam around the farmyard while the others watch from the open barn door.

Stormy Waves

Instead of leaving it stationary, move this stormy scene from side to side slightly so as to give your audience a realistically seasick feeling. Animals such as the sea cow, shark, crab, and hermit crab might all make brief appearances among the wind-tossed waves.

Bright Sunshine

 After storms, sunshine... You could use this frame to make a fierce sun beat down on the desert, or to cast some rays into the farmyard, or the meadow scene.

Moon and Stars

The moon and stars make any of the scenes instantly nighttime. Be careful when cutting out this screen, though: the bars connecting the different elements to the main frame are narrow and quite fragile.

Stormy Weather

Heavy rainclouds and lightning bring a savage storm to any landscape. Shaking a thin metal sheet will create a thunderous roar to go with the lightning flash, and a little gravel shaken in a water glass will sound like sharp rattles of hail. You could make shadow animals hide or flee the scene altogether while the storm rages, then bring them timidly out again as the storm fades and the sun returns.

Rain

This unusual screen is laborious to cut out but effective in action. The main body of the card is removed, leaving just thin, undulating strips running from top to bottom of the frame. Make sure that the screen is far enough away from the secondary light source to keep the stripes indistinct on the wall, and shake the frame up and down slightly—the result will be the convincing appearance of a heavy shower of rain.

City Rooftops

The seated cat is the king of the rooftop vista, and is challenged only by a variety of birds—starling, pigeons, and dove may all pass by him as he surveys his landscape. As the birds leave, you could bring out the moon and stars to suggest that night has fallen.

Country Meadow

 This is a small-scale landscape for some of the more modest animals in your repertoire—the larger and more majestic types have already been given whole jungles and forests as their stage. Try creating a slow, calm, bucolic scenario in which a snail can slide across the grass, and a butterfly can hover above. Birds can pass across the screen, while rabbits and hares enjoy the sunshine.

River Boat Scene

A tranquil bend in the river, flanked by bulrushes and a sailing boat, makes a particularly good setting for various shadow birds—try a gliding swan, a quacking duck, or a swooping swallow. A rabbit or a mouse might also be seen by the vegetation on the right.

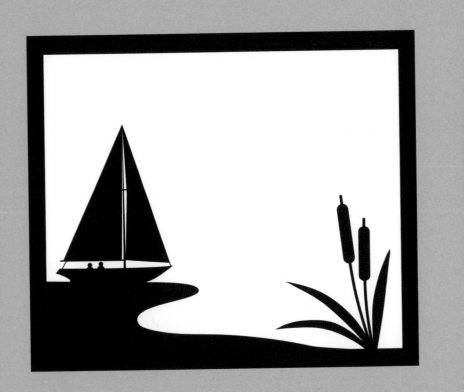

Human Characters

The following pages offer eight shadow characters to extend your repertoire. The elderly man and the lady in the bonnet are probably the simplest to make, and all of the shadows can be pressed into a variety of roles.

Elderly Man

This benign shadow can be used whenever a wise elder character is needed. The beard adds gravitas, and the man can play the part of a wise hermit in the forest, a sea captain looking out onto a rough ocean, or any number of other roles. If he needs to express strong emotion, move the joined fingers of your left hand to make his beard wag in agitation.

Lady in Bonnet

As formed here, the profile of the lady looks quite elderly and can be used for any older character. By tucking the ring finger of your right hand further in, her sharp nose becomes retrousse, and the chin can be made less prominent by curling in your left thumb a little further than shown. Suddenly you have a much younger profile—and the same basic shadow can be used for a variety of characters—for example, she can be both Red Riding Hood and her grandmother. All you will need to add is a wolf (*see pages 196–197*).

Surprised Face

This face can belong to a man or a woman—what characterizes it is its expression of surprise, with open mouth and dropped chin. Although this is an easy shadow to make, it is hard to move realistically, so it is most useful kept as a shadow to "react" to an event on the stage—a trumpeting elephant, perhaps, or a snapping crocodile.

King

 A king can be useful in telling all sorts of tales, and this profile is recognizable from the prominent crown, which is a straightforward shadow to make. You can create a cartoonish effect with exaggerated features by extending the little and middle fingers of your right hand, or fold them in at the knuckle for a more lifelike appearance. Open and close the gap between the little finger and ring finger of your right hand if your king needs to make a pronouncement.

Farmer

The menagerie boasts a whole farmyard of animals, so you may need a farmer to look after them. This character has a flat cap with a long peak and unkempt whiskers (which can be made into a neater beard simply by pulling the three extended fingers of your left hand together into a cleaner outline). Bend the forefinger of your left hand in a little if you want to give the farmer a less exaggerated nose.

Hiawatha

Hiawatha has an impressive tall headdress, similar to that of the cockatoo animal shadow (*see pages 142–143*). If you want to show him hunting in the forest, you can make him look around in an alert way by gently moving the forefinger of your left hand in and out of the gap that forms his eye. If you move the shadow forward slowly and carefully, he will appear to be creeping stealthily through the forest.

Clown

The characteristically flopping hat is easily formed with the forefinger and thumb of your left hand, but the clown's comically jutting chin and nose are quite hard to make accurately; they call for a flexible right hand for the complicated knotting of the fingers required. When you have mastered it, you will find it relatively simple to make the clown "talk" by opening and closing the pairs of fingers.

Laughing Face

Like the surprised face (*see pages 274–275*), this is a useful shadow for reacting to events on stage. The cheerful behatted profile might belong to a member of the audience at the circus, or be simply laughing at the antics of a procession of animals—the snorting pig, the leaping squirrel, or the barking terrier. Also like the surprised-face shadow, this is a difficult shape to animate, so is best formed and then held still.

Index and Resources

A

albatross 102–103
alpaca 120–121
animals, advanced 195–223
animals, challenging 123–193
animals, for single hands, 17–34
animals, for two hands, 37–121
anteater 156–157
antelope 168–169
arcade frame 234–235
armadillo 54–55

B

badger 174–175
basic shapes 12–13
bear 128–129
bear cub 62–63
billy goat 46–47
boar, wild 148–149
bull 92–93
bulldog 146–147
butterfly 106–107

C

camel 216–217
cat 188–189
chameleon 182–183
circus frame 248–249
city rooftops frame 262–263
clown 282–283
cobra, king 158–159
cockatoo 142–143
cockerel 190–191
cougar 152–153
country meadow frame 264–265
cow 94–95
coyote 198–199
crab 50–51
crab, hermit 66–67
crocodile 12–13, 58–59
crow 134–135

D

deer, moose 116–117
deer, red 86–87
deer, roe 88–89
desert frame 244–245

dog, bulldog 146–147
dog, German Shepherd 12–13, 44–45
dog, pug 214–215
dog, terrier 218–219
donkey 178–179
dove 42–43
duck 28–29

E

eagle 162–163
elderly man 270–271
elephant 12–13, 132–133
extending your repertoire 225–267, 270–285

F

face, laughing 284–285
face, surprised 274–275
farmer 278–279
farmyard frame 250–251
fawn 82–83
finger exercises 10–11
forest frame 240–241
fox 104–105

frames and scenery
226, 232–267
frames and scenery, how
to use 9, 232–233
frog 118–119

G
German Shepherd dog
12–13, 44–45
giraffe, adult 70–71
giraffe, baby 24–25
goat 46–47, 184–185
goose 20–21
greyhound 30–31

H
hand and finger exercises
10–11
hare 164–165
hen, roosting 68–69
hermit crab 66–67
Hiawatha 280–281
hills frame 238–239
hippopotamus 114–115
horse 48–49

J
jackal 72–73
jaguar 208–209
jellyfish 40–41
jungle frame 242–243

K
kangaroo 170–171
king 276–277

L
lady in bonnet 272–273
laughing face 284–285
leopard 126–127
lion 206–207
llama 138–139
lyre bird 180–181

M
man, elderly 270–271
marmot 192–193
meadow frame 264–265
mole 160–161
monkey 34–35
moon and stars frame
256–257
moose 116–117
mouse 200–201

N
nanny goat 184–185

O
ostrich 64–65
owl 154–155

P
panther 220–221
parrot 80–81
peacock 144–145
penguin 76–77
people 268–285
pig 130–131
pigeon 112–113
porcupine 74–75

possum 140–141
pug dog 214–215

R
rabbit 124–125
rain frame 260–261
rat 84–85
raven 108–109
red deer 86–87
rhinoceros 202–203
river boat scene frame
266–267
roe deer 88–89
rooftops frame 262–263

S
salamander 22–23
scenery and frames 226,
232–267
scenery and frames, how
to use 9, 232–233
sea anemone 212–213
sea cow 150–151
seashore frame 246–247
shark 38–39
sheep 166–167
showing your shadows
8–9
skunk 78–79
snail 60–61
snake 32–33
snake, king cobra
158–159
sound effects 226–231
sparrow 26

spider 100–101
squirrel 210–211
starling 26–27
stormy waves frame 252–253
stormy weather frame 258–259
sunshine frame 254–255
surprised face 274–275
swallow 18–19
swan 56–57

T

tapir 172–173
terrier 218–219
tiger 204–205
toad 110–111
tortoise 176–177
trees frame 236–237
tropical jungle frame 242–243
turkey 90–91
turtle 98–99

U

unicorn 222–223

V

vulture 136–137

W

water buffalo 96–97
weasel 52–53
wild boar 148–149
wolf 196–197
woodpecker 186–187

Resources

The range of books on shadow art generally is not wide, but the following include non-animal shadows—profiles of famous people, or shadows of human "characters," which you can use to broaden your repertoire:

The Art of Hand Shadows, Albert Almoznino, Dover, 1970

Hand Shadows, Tobar, 1997 (a reprint of *Shadowgraphs Anyone Can Make*, first published in 1927)

Fun With Hand Shadows, Sati Achath, Contemporary Books, 1996